fun at
CHRISTMAS

fun with
CHRISTMAS

PETRA BOASE

PHOTOGRAPHY BY MARK WOOD

50 FANTASTIC FESTIVE PROJECTS FOR KIDS TO MAKE THEMSELVES

southwater

For Uppy, my brilliant flatmate

This edition is published by Southwater

Distributed in the UK by
The Manning Partnership
251–253 London Road East
Batheaston
Bath BA1 7RL
tel. 01225 852 727
fax 01225 852 852

Published in the USA by
Anness Publishing Inc.
27 West 20th Street
Suite 504
New York
NY 10011
fax 212 807 6813

Distributed in Canada by
General Publishing
895 Don Mills Road
400–402 Park Centre
Toronto, Ontario M3C 1W3
tel. 416 445 3333
fax 416 445 5991

Distributed in Australia by
Sandstone Publishing
Unit 1, 360 Norton Street
Leichhardt
New South Wales 2040
tel. 02 9560 7888
fax 02 9560 7488

Southwater is an imprint of Anness Publishing Limited
Hermes House, 88–89 Blackfriars Road, London SE1 8HA
tel. 020 7401 2077; fax 020 7633 9499

© 1998, 2000, 2001 Anness Publishing Limited

Previously published as *Step-by-step 50 Christmas Crafts for Kids*

Publisher: Joanna Lorenz
Project Editors: Sophy Friend and Sarah Ainley
Designer: Colin Hawes
Stylist: Susan Bull
Production Controller: Joanna King

3 5 7 9 10 8 6 4 2

The author would like to thank Isabel Stanley and Ken Eardley for their project work and their help
and expertise in the studio. She would also like to thank Sue Bull for her styling and Mark Wood for his photography.

Contents

INTRODUCTION

If you always worry about what presents to give your friends and family at Christmas, this book is the perfect solution to all your problems. There are lots of exciting gift-wraps, cards, decorations and gifts to make, so leave your savings where they are and get creative!

To avoid running out of time, it's always a good idea to plan ahead and start making your presents early. When you have read through the book and decided what presents and decorations you want to make, study the equipment and materials lists carefully to check what basic items you need. Don't worry if you can't find exactly the same materials as appear in each project; the best part about making your own presents is that there is so much to choose from that you can pick the shapes and colours that you like the best!

Once you have caught the craft bug, a handy tip is to start a recycling box or bag and fill it with useful odds and ends that can be used in the projects, for example, jam jars, cereal boxes, old wrapping paper, empty toilet paper tubes, corks and sweet (candy) wrappers.

You will be able to make a lot of the projects by yourself, but you will need adult help for some of them, so be sure to ask when the project says to do so.

When you have finished making all your presents and decorations, store them in a safe place away from prying eyes, until it is Christmas Day.

Materials

These are some of the materials used in the projects in this book. Some you will already have, others you may have to buy.

Artificial gemstones
These look like jewels and can be glued on to projects for an added touch of sparkle.

Beads
Beads can be made from wood, plastic, metal or glass. They can be glued or sewn on.

Bells
These can be bought from craft shops or large department stores and make a festive jingling sound.

Braids
Braid comes in many widths and can be glued or sewn on.

Buttons
These can be used for decoration and can be glued or sewn on.

Cardboard tubes
These can be found in the middle of rolls of tin foil and toilet paper.

Christmas cards
These can be cut up and glued on to a whole range of projects.

Coloured paper
This paper is very useful! It comes in different thicknesses and colours, and is available from most stationers and art shops.

Corrugated cardboard
Corrugated cardboard has ridges and comes in many thicknesses.

Cotton sewing thread
Thread is used for sewing fabric together. Always try to match the colours of your sewing thread and your fabric.

Cotton wool
This can be used on decorations and cards. It is easily available from supermarkets and chemists.

Doily
This is a lace-like paper, sometimes with a top layer of gold or silver foil. It is useful for making a snowflake effect.

Elastic
Elastic comes in many different widths and strengths.

Embroidery thread (floss)
This is a thick, strong thread which comes in a wide variety of colours.

Enamel paint
This type of paint gives good coverage and can be used to paint both plastic and metal.

Felt
Felt is easy to cut and will not fray. It is available from art and craft shops in a variety of colours.

Foil sweet (candy) wrappers
These give a shiny decorative effect to gifts and ornaments. Remember to save the wrappers whenever you have some sweets (candies).

Glitter
Glitter always adds a Christmassy touch to projects. Take care not to spill your glitter on the floor!

Glitter glue
This is a ready-made mix of glitter and clear glue. It makes decorating projects very easy.

Jam jars
These are useful containers for storing sequins and gemstones.

Letter and number transfers
Transfers can be bought from art shops. They are an easy way of making sure you have neatly written words and numbers.

Metallic foil
This can be bought from art and craft shops. It is thicker than tin foil but can be cut with scissors.

Mini pom-poms
These can be bought from art and craft shops, or you can easily make your own at home.

Modelling clay
This is great for making moulded shapes. It comes in lots of colours.

Neoprene
This is a special fabric that is like a soft rubber. It is easy to cut and glue on to projects for decoration.

Paints
There are many different types of paint, such as fabric, acrylic, poster and watercolour. Always paint in a well-ventilated area.

Paper baubles (styrofoam balls)
These are very light and can be painted and decorated to make fun decorations. Buy them from art and craft shops.

Pine cones
Look out for these the next time you go for a walk near woodland, or buy them from a florist's shop.

Ribbon
This comes in a variety of colours, textures and widths. It can be tied in pretty bows and wrapped around presents, or use it for hanging decorations.

Rope
This is thicker and stronger than string. Glue rope on to a block of wood and use as a printing block.

Sequins
These shiny decorations can be glued or sewn on to paper, cardboard or fabric.

Squeezy paint
This is great for decorating projects and you may find it easier to use than an ordinary paintbrush for painting small details and patterns.

Sticky-backed plastic (contact paper)
This has a paper backing, so that after you have cut out your shape, you can peel the backing off and stick the shape in place.

Tinsel
A Christmas favourite which can be cut up and used to decorate many projects.

Tissue paper
This is a delicate, transparent paper. It is available in many colours and can be used in lots of ways for decoration.

Wool (yarn)
This comes in many different colours and is available from department stores or craft shops.

tinsel

pine cones

cardboard tubes

jar

enamel paint

squeezy paint

braids

mini pom-poms

rope

bells

poster paints

glitter glue

wool (yarn)

beads

glitter

corrugated cardboard

metallic foil

embroidery thread (floss)

tissue paper

ribbon

cotton sewing thread

elastic

modelling clay

coloured paper

neoprene

artificial gemstones

metallic foil

Christmas cards

felt

buttons

scourer pad (sponge)

sequins

aaaaaaa
ccccddd
eeeeeef
hhhhhiii

transfers

paper bauble (styrofoam ball)

sweet (candy) wrappers

doily

cotton wool

corks

sticky-backed plastic (contact paper)

Equipment

This is a range of the equipment used in this book. You will probably have many items, but it may be worth buying one or two new tools.

Badge findings
These are glued or sewn on to the back of badges. They can be bought from specialist shops.

Compass
A very useful tool for drawing different sized circles with.

Corks
Corks are useful to dab into paint and then print with.

Double-sided sticky tape
A type of tape that is sticky on both sides.

Earring findings
These are glued on to the back of earrings so that they can then be clipped on to your ears.

Eraser
An eraser is useful for rubbing out any pencilled markings you may have made.

Fabric scissors
These sharp scissors are used to cut fabric. They should always be handled with care.

Felt-tip pens
Felt-tip pens are useful for drawing around templates.

Foam roller
These are taken from ordinary hair rollers. They are very good for printing dots. Wash the roller each time you use a new colour.

Glue stick
A glue stick is less messy than most other types of glue. This type shows up as a purple colour

until it dries so that you can see where you are gluing. It is used for sticking paper to paper.

Gold pen
A special effect pen that can be used for writing messages in cards and for decorating paper.

Hair clip (barrette)
Hair clips (barrettes) can be bought from specialist craft shops. They can be decorated with fabric or neoprene. You will need to use a strong glue to stick the materials on to the clip.

Hole punch
This is used for punching holes in paper or cardboard.

Knife
Use this sharp tool for cutting. Always cut onto a firm surface and ask an adult to help you.

Needles
These have a very sharp point and are used in sewing projects. Ask an adult to help you if you need to use a needle.

Paintbrushes
These come in a variety of thicknesses. Store your brushes with the bristles facing upwards.

Palette
A palette is useful for mixing paint. If you don't have one, an old saucer is just as good.

Paper fasteners
These are used for holding two pieces of paper together so the top piece can spin around.

Paper scissors
These are used for cutting paper, cardboard or metallic foil. They should be of the type that are made specially for children and have rounded blades.

Pencil
A soft pencil is useful for making tracings and transferring them to cardboard and paper.

Pencil sharpener
This is useful for sharpening lead and coloured pencils.

Pinking shears
When you cut fabric or paper with these scissors you get an attractive crinkly edge.

Pins
These are sharp and are used for pinning pieces of fabric together.

PVA (white) glue
Always use a non-toxic glue and work in a well-ventilated area. PVA (white) glue is good for gluing cardboard and fabric.

Ring finding
This can be glued to the back of a small project to turn it into a ring. Use a strong glue to stick the materials on to the ring back.

Safety pins
These are useful for holding pieces of material together, or for taping to the back of badges.

Sandpaper
Rub wood and glazed ceramics with sandpaper, to make the surface smooth for painting.

Scourer pad (sponge)
This is ideal for cutting into shapes to make printing blocks.

Single hole punch
This can be used for punching single holes in paper, cardboard, neoprene or felt.

Sponge
Lightly dip a sponge into paint and sponge over a stencil, or use it to make prints.

Sticky tape
This can be used for sticking paper, cardboard and foil.

Strong glue
Always use a non-toxic and solvent-free glue. Strong glue is useful for sticking heavier cardboard together.

Tracing paper
This is a lightweight transparent paper. It is used to trace and transfer templates and designs.

Varnish
Always use a non-toxic, water-based varnish and work in a well-ventilated area. Varnish is used to protect a wooden surface that has been decorated with paint or pieces of paper or cardboard.

Water container
This is a special container with a safety lid. If you don't have one, a clean jam jar is just as good.

Wood
Glue a length of string in a coil on a block of wood, to make a printing block.

PVA (white) glue

hole punch

strong glue

sandpaper

wood

glue stick

single bole
punch

compass

paintbrushes

foam roller

tracing paper

palette

scourer pad
(sponge)

water container

hair clip
(barrette)

badge
finding

ring finding

safety pin

sponge

earring
findings

pencil

felt-tip pen

gold pen

ballpoint pen

badge findings

needles

pins

pencil
sharpener

paper
fasteners

eraser

varnish

fabric
scissors

knife

ruler

pinking
shears

paper
scissors

double-sided
sticky tape

TECHNIQUES

Tracing

Some of the projects in this book have patterns that you can transfer directly to paper or use to make templates. Tracing is the quickest way to make copies of a pattern so that you can easily transfer it to another piece of paper or cardboard.

1 Lay your piece of tracing paper on the pattern and use a soft pencil to draw over the image, making a dark line.

2 Turn the sheet of tracing paper over and place it on a scrap of paper. Scribble over the lines with your pencil.

3 Turn the tracing right-side up again and place it on an appropriate piece of paper or cardboard. Carefully draw over the lines to transfer the tracing to the paper or cardboard. Lift up the tracing paper and you will see that your outline is now on the paper or cardboard.

Scaling-up

Sometimes you will want to make a project bigger than the template given and will need to scale-up the size of the template. It is very easy to make a template bigger – all you need is a piece of plain paper, a pencil and a ruler. You could use a photocopier instead, if you prefer.

1 Trace the template and transfer it to a sheet of paper. Draw a box around the template. Draw two diagonal lines through the box, from each of the bottom corners.

2 Draw a box for the new image on the same piece of paper. Make the box as large as you want your scaled-up image to be. Draw two diagonal lines through the new box, as before.

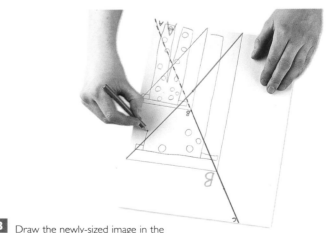

3 Draw the newly-sized image in the box, looking very carefully at the original.

Folding Paper

Paper can be folded in a variety of ways to great effect. One of the simplest methods is to fold a sheet of paper into sections like a concertina. You can hang the finished design as a decoration.

1 Fold two sheets of paper in contrasting colours into sections about 2.5 cm (1 in) wide.

2 Fold each piece of paper in the middle to make a semi-circle. Join the two ends together with a staple.

3 With the help of an adult, join the two semi-circles together at the outside edges to form a circle.

Flattening and Cutting up a Box

Cardboard is used for many of the projects in this book. Old boxes are the best source of cardboard, and you can flatten them out easily.

1 Remove any tape that is holding the box together and press the box flat.

2 Cut the box into pieces, ready for use in your various projects.

Re-using Foil Wrappers

Coloured foil is great for decorations, and you don't have to buy it specially. Save old sweet (candy) wrappers made of pretty colours, and cut them into different shapes.

1 Flatten the sweet (candy) wrappers and chocolate cases and smooth them out with your hands. Cut up the wrappers and use as decorations for your projects. Sweet wrappers and chocolate cases are always cheerful and will make your projects look really festive!

Using a Compass

This is an old-fashioned instrument that is still one of the best tools you can use to draw neat circles. You will also need a freshly sharpened pencil.

1 Place the point of the compass on the piece of paper or cardboard that you want to draw the circle on. The point of the compass is sharp so be careful when you use it.

2 Decide on how large you need your circle to be and pull out the arm of the compass. Place the pencil on the surface and, holding the top of the compass, draw the circle.

Mixing Paints

If you only have the basic primary colours (red, yellow and blue) of paint, try mixing them together to make new colours.

1 Mix yellow and blue paints together to make green. For a bright green use mainly yellow paint.

2 Mix yellow and red paints together to make orange. For a dark orange use mainly red paint.

Saving Glitter

This handy tip shows you how to save glitter and avoid making a mess.

1 Fold a scrap of paper in half and then open it out and lay it under the project you are working on. When you have sprinkled the glitter over the project, fold the paper in half again and place the end of the paper by the crease over the glitter tube and carefully pour it back into the tube.

3 Mix blue and red paints together to make purple. For a deep royal purple use mainly blue paint.

Fixing Jewellery Findings

These are small metal attachments that are glued on to the back of your projects to turn them into pieces of jewellery. The findings should be glued on with strong glue.

1 This is a brooch or badge finding. Let the glue harden completely before pinning the badge on to your clothes. For clip-on earring findings, when you glue them on to your project, open them out and keep them open until the glue has hardened. With an adjustable ring finding, simply squeeze the two metal sides together to make it smaller or pull them out gently to make it larger.

Curling

Thin strips of paper can be pulled with a pencil to create gentle curls. The curls are especially good for adding extra decoration to your wrapped Christmas presents.

1 Cut thin strips of paper about 1 cm (½ in) wide. Holding a strip of paper in one hand, pull a pencil down its length several times. Don't pull too hard or you'll tear the paper. The paper will form gentle curls. To make tighter curls, roll the strips around a pencil.

Using a Hole Punch

This is a single hole punch which can be bought from specialist craft shops or large department stores. It is useful for making holes and polka-dots.

1 Punch through felt to make holes or neat mini dots which can then be glued on to other surfaces.

2 If you want to make a lot of paper dots at one time, fold a piece of paper in half and then in half again and punch through it.

3 When you have made a gift tag, punch a hole at one end of it so that you can thread a piece of ribbon or string through it.

TEMPLATES

You will need templates for some of the
projects in this book. Trace the templates
directly from the page, or enlarge them to
the size required, following the instructions
given at the beginning of the book.

Festive Fabric Card

Christmas Pom-Poms

Starry Gift-wrap and Tag

Christmas Tree Card and Tag

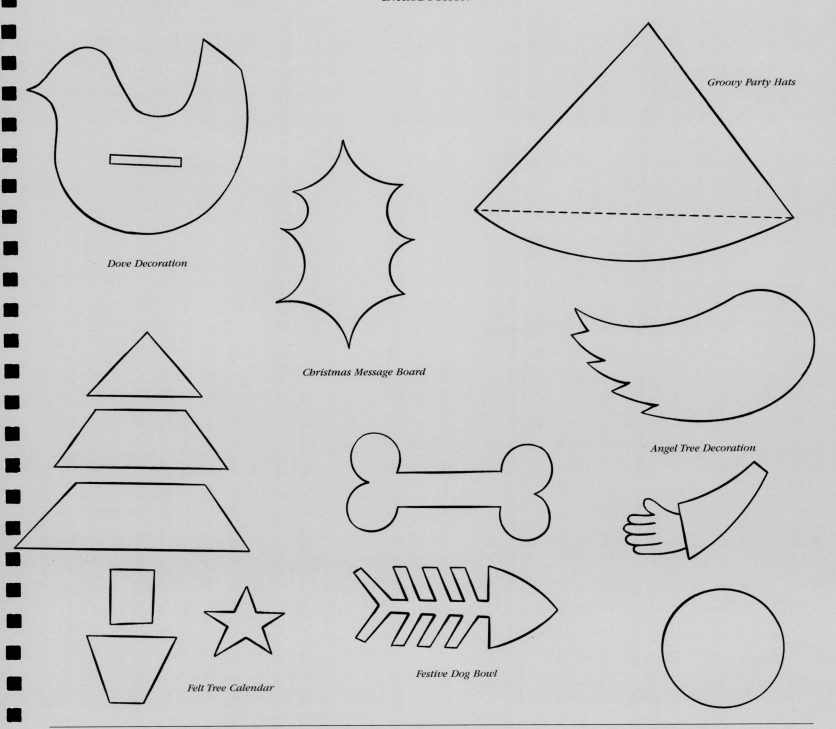

Dove Decoration

Christmas Message Board

Groovy Party Hats

Angel Tree Decoration

Felt Tree Calendar

Festive Dog Bowl

Appliquéd Photo Album

Party Badges

*Holly Leaf
Picture Frame*

Mini Gift bags

Stained Glass Card

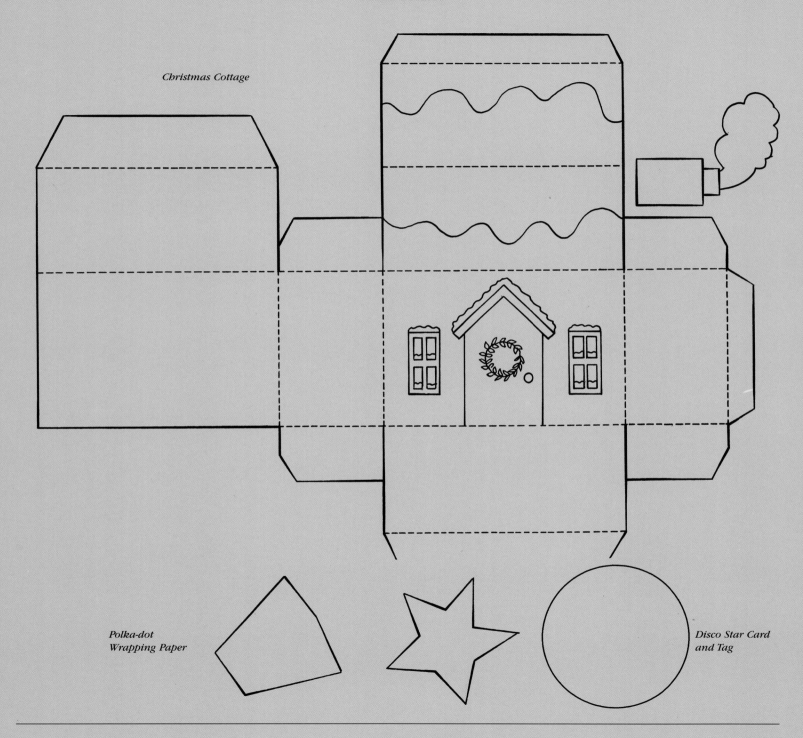

Christmas Cottage

Polka-dot
Wrapping Paper

Disco Star Card
and Tag

Tin Heart and Star
Tree Decorations

Advent Table Decoration

Snowman Card

Wintry Scarf and
Gloves

Christmas Tree Earrings

Wintry Scarf and Gloves

*Christmas Pudding
Apron*

Mini Tree Stockings

GIFT-WRAPS AND CARDS

Festive Fabric Card

This charming little cat is all dressed up for Christmas! If you like the design so much that you do not want to give it as a festive card, put it into a frame, sign it and give it to someone as a present.

YOU WILL NEED
coloured cardboard
felt-tip pen
paper scissors
felt squares in various colours
fabric scissors
single hole punch
PVA (white) glue
squeezy paints in various colours
artificial gemstone

PVA (white) glue

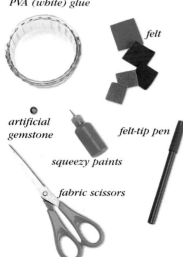

felt

artificial gemstone

felt-tip pen

squeezy paints

fabric scissors

1 Fold the sheet of cardboard in half. Use a felt-tip pen to trace the templates from this book, then cut them out using paper scissors. Use the felt-tip pen to draw around the templates on the reverse side of the pieces of felt.

2 Use the fabric scissors to cut all of the cat shapes and the pieces for the snowy background out of the felt. Always remember to save any leftover scraps of fabric for other projects.

3 Punch lots of dots from a piece of white felt, using the single hole punch. These white dots will be used to make the snow that is falling around the cat.

4 Position all of the felt shapes on the background felt and, when you are happy with how they look, glue them in place with PVA (white) glue.

5 Using squeezy paints, decorate the cat's face to give it eyes, whiskers and a smile. If you find this too difficult, use felt-tip pens instead. Glue an artificial gemstone on the cat's collar.

6 Paint a few dabs of glue on the reverse side of the fabric design and glue it firmly in place on to the folded sheet of cardboard. Alternatively, use it as a picture and place it in a frame.

Polka-dot Wrapping Paper

You will have great fun stamping and printing to make this gift-wrap. This project uses a sponge roller and a cork to print with. Be adventurous and see what else you can use to make a printed shape.

YOU WILL NEED
coloured paper
small roller sponge
poster paints in various colours
cork
scourer pad (sponge)
scissors
single hole punch
string

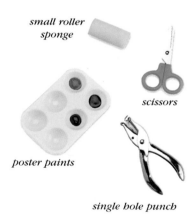

small roller sponge

scissors

poster paints

single hole punch

1 Lay the coloured paper on a flat, well-covered surface. Dab the end of the roller sponge in one of the paint colours. Carefully stamp dots on the paper to make a triangle shape for the Christmas tree. You may need to add more paint to the roller between prints.

2 Dab a cork in a different colour of paint and print a line of dots under the tree to make the tree trunk.

3 Cut a scourer pad (sponge) to look like a tree stand. Dab the scourer pad in a new paint colour and print it under the tree trunk.

4 To make a tag, dab a scrap piece of scourer pad in paint and print a star shape on cardboard. When dry, cut around the shape. Punch a hole in the top of the tag and thread with string.

Rope-printed Paper

This design is simple but looks very stylish. If you don't have any wood to make the printing block, you can use a piece of thick cardboard instead.

YOU WILL NEED
wooden block
pencil
PVA (white) glue
paintbrush
thin rope
poster paint
scissors
coloured paper
single hole punch
ribbon

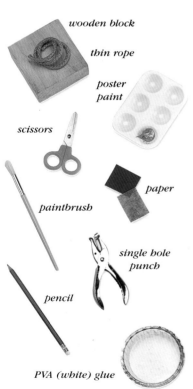

wooden block
thin rope
poster paint
scissors
paper
paintbrush
single hole punch
pencil
PVA (white) glue

1 Draw a spiral shape on a block of wood, using a pencil so that you can rub out any mistakes. Paint a coat of PVA (white) glue over the spiral shape.

2 Begin laying the rope in place before the glue dries. Starting in the centre of the spiral, carefully wind the rope around, following the spiral design. Hold the rope in place as you work, so that it does not spring off.

3 Make sure you are working on a well-covered surface before you start to paint. Cover the rope generously with paint and then stamp the design on the paper. You will need to repaint the rope for each print you make.

4 Make a gift tag to go with the paper. Print the design on coloured paper. When the paint is dry, cut around the design and punch a hole in the edge. Pull a length of ribbon through the hole for attaching the tag to a present.

Christmas Tree Card

Scourer pads (sponges) are usually used for cleaning pots and pans in the kitchen, but they can also be cut into shapes and used to decorate Christmas cards.

YOU WILL NEED
coloured cardboard
pencil
scissors
scourer pads (sponges) in various
    colours
pins
single hole punch
sequins
glitter glue
PVA (white) glue
ribbon

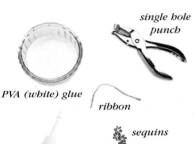

single hole punch

PVA (white) glue

ribbon

sequins

glitter glue

scissors

scourer pads (sponges)

coloured cardboard

paint brush

1 Fold the piece of coloured cardboard in half. Trace the templates from this book and cut them out with a pair of scissors. Lay the templates on the different coloured scourer pads (sponges) and pin them in place to make them easier to cut out.

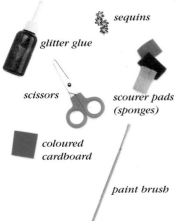

2 Carefully cut around the templates, using a pair of scissors, then remove the pins. You should now have a Christmas tree and a Christmas tree stand.

3 Punch holes out of the tree stand. Punch dots out of a scrap of scourer pad in a contrasting colour to the tree stand. Place the dots in the holes on the tree stand.

4 Decorate the tree with sequins and glitter glue, and when the glue has dried, glue the tree on to the folded piece of card. Using the same method, make a gift tag to match.

Paper Mosaic Gift Box

This glitzy box looks like a miniature treasure chest and is terrific for any presents you find too difficult to wrap in paper. If you can't find a small box, decorate an old shoe box instead.

YOU WILL NEED
shiny papers in various colours
scissors
cardboard box, sprayed silver if
  liked
paintbrush
PVA (white) glue
glitter glue

PVA (white) glue

cardboard box

glitter glue

scissors

shiny coloured papers

coloured cardboard

paintbrush

1 Cut up lots of strips of paper from the shiny coloured papers and then cut some of the strips into small squares. The bigger your box, the more strips and squares you will need.

2 Glue the squares on to the lid of the box, leaving a small gap in between each of the squares. Continue until you have covered the whole of the box lid.

3 Glue the strips of paper all around the sides of the box, leaving small gaps between each strip. Leave the lid and box until the glue is completely dry.

4 Carefully apply the glitter glue on the lid of the box where the gaps are. Leave it to dry: it takes quite a long time to set. If you don't have any glitter glue, use ordinary glitter and glue instead.

Three Kings Gift-wrap

Using a humble potato to print with is an easy way to create your own gift-wrap. This jewelled crown design will add a regal touch to your presents.

YOU WILL NEED
pencil
scissors
coloured cardboard
potato
knife
felt-tip pen
paper towels
squeezy paints in various colours
glitter glue

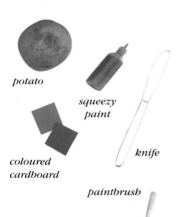

potato

squeezy paint

coloured cardboard

knife

paintbrush

1 Trace the crown template from this book and cut it out with a pair of scissors. With the help of an adult, use a knife to cut a potato in half. Draw around the crown template on one half of the potato with a felt-tip pen.

2 With the help of an adult, cut out the area around the crown shape. It is important that the shape is cut out as neatly as possible, so that the potato gives a nicely shaped print.

3 Squeeze a large dab of paint on a thick pad of paper towels for dipping the potato into.

4 Gently dip the potato in the paint. You can add paint directly on to the potato shape if you prefer. Carefully stamp the potato on the paper to make a print. Slowly remove the potato to reveal the print you have made.

5 Use a paper towel to tidy up the printing area of the potato before you apply more paint on the paper towels or directly on to the potato. Continue printing crown shapes until you have covered the paper. Let the paint dry.

6 Add your own decoration to the printed crowns with squeezy paints and let dry. For a finishing touch, add a few dabs of glitter glue.

Disco Star Card and Tag

Use up your scraps of coloured paper and cardboard to make this groovy spinning star card and matching gift tag.

YOU WILL NEED
pencil
coloured cardboard
scissors
coloured paper
PVA (white) glue
paintbrush
paper fasteners
single hole punch
ribbon

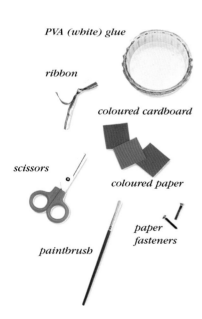

PVA (white) glue

ribbon

coloured cardboard

scissors

coloured paper

paintbrush

paper fasteners

1 Trace the star and circle templates from this book and cut them out with a pair of scissors. Draw round the star template on different coloured pieces of cardboard and cut out the star shapes. Draw round the circle template on each of the pieces of card and cut out the circles.

2 Cut a piece of cardboard to the size you want your card to be and fold it in half. Glue the paper circles on to the front side of the card.

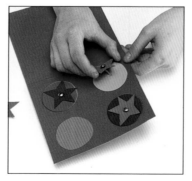
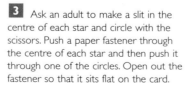

3 Ask an adult to make a slit in the centre of each star and circle with the scissors. Push a paper fastener through the centre of each star and then push it through one of the circles. Open out the fastener so that it sits flat on the card.

4 Make a gift tag to match the card. Punch a hole at one end of the tag to thread a piece of ribbon through.

Stained Glass Card

To enjoy the full beauty of this card you need to open it up and position it by a window. When the sun shines the light will stream through the tissue paper and light up the Christmas tree.

YOU WILL NEED
scissors
black cardboard
crayon or pencil
tissue paper in various colours
paintbrush
PVA (white) glue and
    paper glue stick
glitter glue

tissue paper

glitter glue

black cardboard

PVA (white) glue

paper glue stick

pencil

scissors

1 Cut a square shape from a piece of black cardboard, fold it in half and press down firmly on the fold. Open out the card. Trace the template from this book and cut it out. Using a crayon or pencil, draw around the template on the left side of the card.

2 With the help of an adult, use a pair of scissors to cut out the Christmas tree from inside the design.

3 Cut out differently coloured pieces of tissue paper, slightly bigger than the openings in the card, and begin gluing them in place on the inside of the card.

4 Continue gluing the pieces of tissue paper, alternating the colours. Allow the glue to dry before closing the card. Decorate with small dabs of glitter glue, if you wish.

Starry Gift-wrap and Tag

To make this paper project you will need to make a star stencil from a piece of stiff cardboard. You can make stencils in other shapes, too. Try out your design first on a piece of scrap paper, to make sure you are happy with it.

YOU WILL NEED
pen or pencil
stiff cardboard
scissors
single hole punch
ribbon or string
sponge
gold paint
shiny papers in various colours
PVA (white) glue

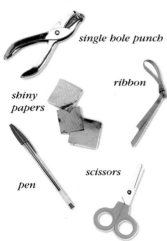

single hole punch

ribbon

shiny papers

scissors

pen

1 Trace the template for the star from this book and draw round it on a piece of stiff cardboard. With the help of an adult, cut out the inside of the star shape, so that you are left with the border as a stencil.

2 Draw round the template to make a star for the gift tag. Cut out the star. Using a single hole punch, punch a hole in the tip of one of the points and thread it with ribbon or string.

3 Dip the sponge in a small amount of paint. Position the stencil on the paper and dab through it with the sponge. Remove the stencil to reveal the print. Re-position the stencil and repeat.

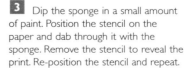

4 When you have covered all of the paper with the stencilled star, cut or punch lots of dots from the shiny papers. Glue a dot on to the points of the stars on the paper, and the tag.

Snowman Card

The lovable seasonal character on this card
is made from pieces of fluffy cotton wool.

YOU WILL NEED
white cotton wool
coloured cardboard
white paper
paintbrush
PVA (white) glue
scissors
coloured papers
single hole punch

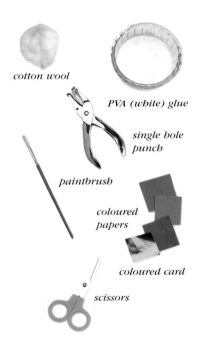

cotton wool

PVA (white) glue

single hole punch

paintbrush

coloured papers

coloured card

scissors

1 Gently mould two pieces of cotton wool into shapes to make the head and body of the snowman. Make sure you make your snowman nice and fat!

2 Fold a piece of cardboard in half, and glue a piece of white paper on the base at the front of the card, to look like a snowdrift. Glue the snowman's head and body on the cardboard.

3 Cut out bits of coloured paper for the snowman's face, hat and scarf and glue them into position.

4 Punch some dots from white paper, using the single hole punch, and glue them on the cardboard around the snowman, to look like gently falling flakes of snow. Leave the glue to dry.

DECORATIONS

Advent Table Decoration

Glue twenty-four sweets (candies) on to this terrific decoration and eat one a day in the countdown to Christmas Day.

YOU WILL NEED
green cardboard
PVA (white) glue
paintbrush
green crêpe paper
foil-wrapped sweets (candies)
pencil
scissors
gold cardboard
corrugated cardboard
terracotta flower pot
red poster paint

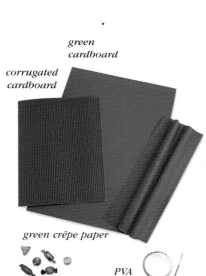

green cardboard

corrugated cardboard

green crêpe paper

foil-wrapped sweets (candies)

PVA (white) glue and paintbrush

1 Roll a piece of green cardboard into a cone shape, using your hands. Glue along one edge of the cardboard, and hold the cone shape in place with your hands until the glue has dried.

2 Tear up lots of pieces of crêpe paper and scrunch them up. Paint glue on one side, and glue them all over the cone. Leave until the glue has dried.

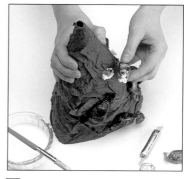

3 Glue the sweets (candies) on to the tree. Hold each sweet in place until the glue has dried.

4 Trace the star template from this book and cut it out. Draw around the template on gold cardboard and cut it out. Make a second star in this way. Cut out a strip of cardboard and place it between the stars. Glue them together.

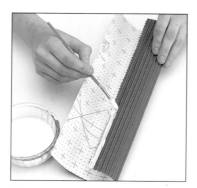

5 Cut a rectangle of corrugated cardboard and roll it up to make a tube. This makes the tree's trunk. Glue along one edge of the tube and hold in place until the glue has dried.

6 Paint a terracotta flower pot with red paint and, when the paint is dry, place the trunk in the pot and balance the tree on top of it. Glue the star on top of the tree.

Sparkly Sequin Baubles

Try decorating these Christmas baubles in as many different ways as you can. You could use foil sweet (candy) wrappers and small artificial gemstones to create other sparkly effects.

YOU WILL NEED
sparkly embroidery thread (floss)
   or wool (yarn)
paper baubles (styrofoam balls)
scissors
PVA (white) glue
paintbrush
poster paints
sequins
glitter glue

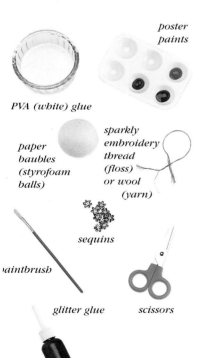

PVA (white) glue

poster paints

paper baubles (styrofoam balls)

sparkly embroidery thread (floss) or wool (yarn)

sequins

paintbrush

glitter glue

scissors

1 Cut a length of sparkly thread and fold it in half to make a loop. Glue the ends of the loop to the top of one of the paper baubles (styrofoam balls). Hold the thread in place with your hands until the glue has dried. Repeat for each of the paper baubles.

2 Paint the baubles with the poster paints. Red, purple and gold paints have been used here but you could use any colours you like. Hang the baubles up by the loops while the paint dries.

3 When the paint has dried, glue a few of the sequins on to each of the baubles. Allow the glue to dry.

4 Using the glitter glue, paint glitter dots in between the sequins and in the middle of the sequins. Leave to dry.

Button Decorations

You can rummage around flea markets for interesting old buttons for this project. If you can't find enough red or green buttons to make these decorations, simply use a mixture of colours.

YOU WILL NEED
felt-tip pen
red and green felt
scissors
needle
sewing thread
red and green buttons
ribbon
PVA (white) glue
paintbrush

PVA (white) glue

sewing thread

ribbon

red and green felt squares

red and green buttons

paintbrush

scissors

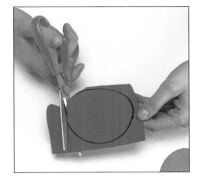

1 Using a felt-tip pen, draw a circle shape on red and green felt. Cut out the shapes and repeat, so that you have several circles in both colours.

2 Thread a needle with sewing thread and sew a selection of green buttons on to the circles of green felt. Sew a selection of red buttons on to the circles of red felt.

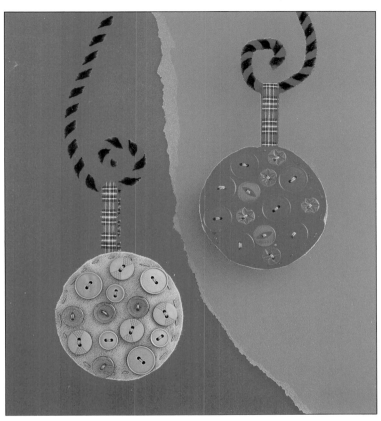

3 Turn over one of the circles of felt and glue on a folded loop of ribbon along one of the edges.

4 Place one green circle on top of one red circle and join together with glue. Sew around the edge of the circles with running stitch. Repeat for any remaining felt circles.

Dove Decoration

These doves look very elegant. You could enlarge the template on a photocopier to make lots of different sized doves to hang on your tree.

YOU WILL NEED
pencil
coloured cardboard
scissors
coloured paper
gold pen
single hole punch
ribbon

gold pen

coloured paper

coloured cardboard

ribbon

scissors

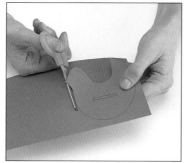

1 Trace the template for the dove's body from this book and cut it out. Draw around the template on to a piece of coloured cardboard. Ask an adult to help you make a slit in the dove's body where the wings will go. Cut out the dove shape.

2 Cut out a rectangle of coloured paper and fold it into a paper fan by turning it over each time you make a fold. This will make the dove's wings.

3 Open out the fan and decorate the edges of the wings with the gold pen. Draw patterns on the dove's body in any way you like. Leave for a few minutes to allow the pen marks to dry.

4 Fold up the fan and pass it through the slit in the dove. Open out the two ends so that they meet above the dove. Hold the two sides of the fan together and punch a hole through the paper. Thread a piece of ribbon through the hole and tie in a knot.

Christmas Pom-poms

These fluffy pom-poms look great hung all over a Christmas tree. They make good use of all your odds and ends of wool (yarn). Use some strands of metallic wool for a gleaming touch.

YOU WILL NEED
pencil
cardboard
scissors
wool (yarn) in various colours

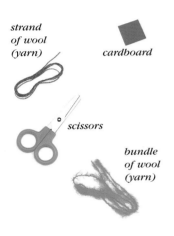

strand of wool (yarn)   *cardboard*

scissors

bundle of wool (yarn)

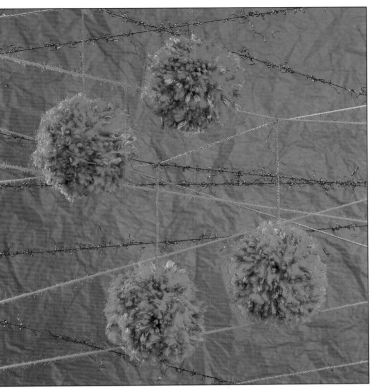

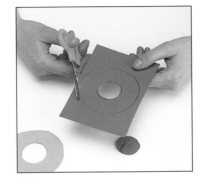

1 Trace the templates from this book and cut them out. Using the templates, draw two circles on cardboard exactly the same size, with one smaller circle in the centre of each. Cut out the circles.

2 Place the two pieces of cardboard together. Tie the end of the wool (yarn) bundle in a knot around the cardboard and thread the wool through the hole. Wrap around the whole circle until the centre hole is almost full. Tuck the ends of the wool in to stop them unravelling.

3 Place one blade of the scissors in between the two pieces of cardboard and carefully cut around the circle, snipping the wool as you go.

4 Wrap a long strand of wool in between the two pieces of cardboard and tie in a knot. Tear off the pieces of cardboard and throw them away. Fluff up the pom-pom and trim any loose ends with a pair of scissors.

Angel Tree Decoration

This decoration will add a beautiful finishing touch to your Christmas tree. If you don't have a tree, place the angel somewhere special, where everyone can see her.

YOU WILL NEED
thin white cardboard
double-sided sticky tape
scissors
silver paper doily
PVA (white) glue
pencil
gold cardboard
small cake candle
paper bauble (styrofoam ball)
paintbrush
poster paints in various colours
yellow wool (yarn)

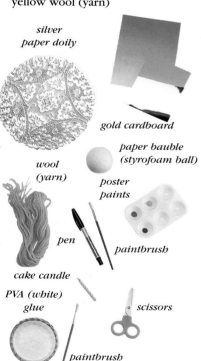

silver paper doily

gold cardboard

paper bauble (styrofoam ball)

wool (yarn)

poster paints

pen

paintbrush

cake candle

PVA (white) glue

scissors

paintbrush

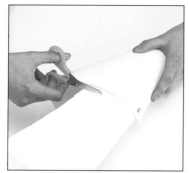

1 Make a cone shape from the thin white cardboard. Stick a strip of double-sided sticky tape under one of the edges, peel off the backing tape and stick it in place. The cone shape will make the body of the angel.

2 Cut a doily to fit around the cone shape and glue it in place. Leave to dry. Trace the templates for the arms, wings and halo and cut them out.

3 For the wings and halo, draw around the templates on gold cardboard. For the arms and hands, draw around the templates on white cardboard. Draw in the fingers yourself with a pencil.

4 When you have cut out the shapes, glue the arms and wings on to the angel's body. Allow the glue to dry. Slot a small cake candle between the angel's hands.

5 Ask an adult to help you stick a pencil into the paper bauble (styrofoam ball). Paint the angel's eyes, nose and mouth on the paper bauble. Leave aside for a few minutes to let the paint dry.

6 Cut about twelve strands of yellow wool (yarn) the same length and glue them to the top of the angel's head as hair. Glue the gold halo to the back of the angel's head. Attach the angel's head to her body.

Gift-wrap Advent Calendar

Instead of buying an Advent calendar this year, why not make your own, using last year's Christmas cards and a sheet of gift-wrap?

YOU WILL NEED
sheet of gift-wrap
ruler
pencil
scissors
assorted Christmas cards
PVA (white) glue
number transfers
ribbon
backing cardboard, cut to the
    same size as the gift-wrap

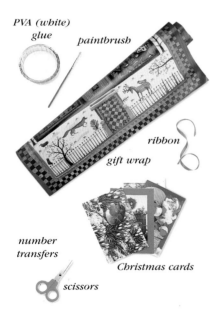

PVA (white)
glue
paintbrush

ribbon

gift wrap

number
transfers

Christmas cards

scissors

1 Carefully mark each of the twenty-four doors on the gift-wrap, using a ruler and pencil. Try to choose pretty areas of the gift-wrap for the positions of the doors. You can make the doors different sizes if you like.

2 Cut out three sides of each door, leaving one side as a hinge so that you can open and shut the door easily.

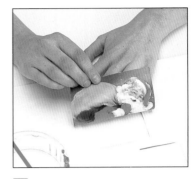

3 Cut out the pictures from some old Christmas cards and glue one picture behind each door. Leave for a few minutes to let the glue dry.

4 Dab a small amount of glue along one edge of each door and close them.

5 Using the number transfers and a pencil, rub a number between one and twenty-four on each door.

6 Cut a piece of ribbon and fold it in half to make a hanging loop. Glue the ends of the loop behind the top edge of the paper. Glue the backing cardboard to the reverse side of the calendar.

Christmas Cottage

You could fill this yuletide cottage with a small gift of tasty homemade fudge or Christmas cookies.

YOU WILL NEED
pencil
scissors
coloured paper
ruler
double-sided sticky tape
paintbrush
poster paints in various colours
PVA (white) glue
silver glitter

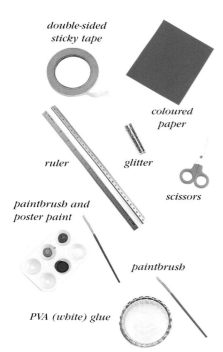

double-sided sticky tape

coloured paper

ruler   glitter

scissors

paintbrush and poster paint

paintbrush

PVA (white) glue

1 Trace the templates for the cottage and chimney and cut them out. Draw around the templates on coloured paper, and lightly mark out the lines of the cottage with a pencil. Use the blunt edge of a pair of scissors to score along the lines. Using a ruler to guide the scissors helps to keep the lines straight.

2 Make folds along the scored lines of the cottage and fold into a box. Place a small piece of double-sided sticky tape along the edges of the four tabs, peel away the backing and stick down firmly. Fold down the roof. Cut the chimney shape out of the paper.

3 Paint on the door and windows and allow the paint to dry. Paint a festive holly wreath on to the front door. Allow the paint to dry. Glue the chimney pot on the roof and allow the glue to dry.

4 Stick the roof down with double-sided tape, so that you can open and close the roof. To finish the cottage, glue a line of glitter on the roof to look like a sprinkling of sparkling snow.

Rudolph the Reindeer Paper Chains

These festive-looking reindeer will look great hung on a wall or around a window. Why not paint each one differently and give them funny faces?

YOU WILL NEED
pencil
coloured paper
scissors
paintbrush
poster paints in various colours
hole punch
paper fasteners

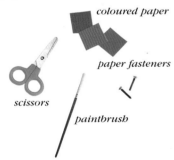

coloured paper

paper fasteners

scissors

paintbrush

hole punch

poster paint

pencil

1 Draw three reindeer head shapes on the coloured paper and cut them out. Draw shapes for the reindeers' antlers and noses and cut them out. For each of the reindeer you will need two antlers, a head and a nose.

2 Paint in the details for the reindeer's face and add patterns on the shapes if you like. Let the paint dry.

3 Mark two points between the reindeers' ears with a pencil. Punch through the marks with a hole punch.

4 Thread a paper fastener through the holes and join the antlers together to make the reindeer chain. Open out the paper fasteners so that they lie flat.

Tin Heart and Star Tree Decorations

Watch these decorations dazzle on your Christmas tree or hang them up by a window to catch the light. You can buy sheets of metallic foil from specialist craft shops.

YOU WILL NEED
pencil
scissors
ballpoint pen
sheets of metallic foil in various
    colours
ruler
single hole punch
ribbon

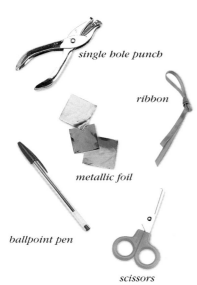

single hole punch

ribbon

metallic foil

ballpoint pen

scissors

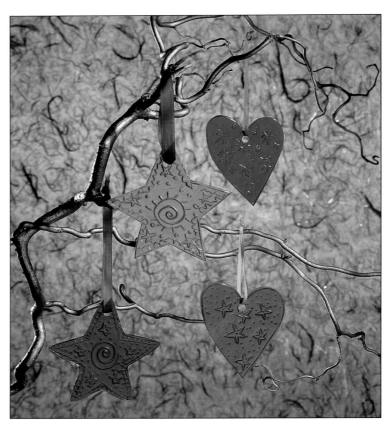

1 Trace the templates from this book and cut them out with a pair of scissors. Using a ballpoint pen, draw around the templates on the reverse of the pieces of metallic foil.

2 Using the ballpoint pen, draw lots of swirly and polka-dot patterns on the reverse side of the metallic foil.

3 Cut out the shapes approximately 3 mm (⅛ in) from the edge of the drawn line. Save any leftover foil for using in other craft projects.

4 Using a single hole punch, punch a hole in each of the decorated shapes and thread a piece of ribbon through. Tie the ends of the ribbon in a knot to make a hanging loop.

Mini Tree Stockings

These cute Christmas stockings add a festive touch to a Christmas tree. Pop a few small gifts or a couple of red and white striped candy canes inside, to make them even more appealing.

YOU WILL NEED
felt-tip pen
scissors
sheets of felt in various colours
PVA (white) glue
paintbrush
needle
sewing thread
ribbon
small bell

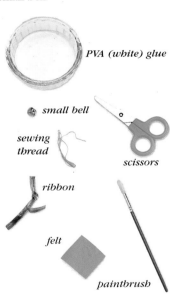

PVA (white) glue

small bell

sewing
thread

scissors

ribbon

felt

paintbrush

1 Trace the mini stocking template from this book and cut it out with a pair of scissors. Draw around the template on two different coloured pieces of felt. Draw some stars and dots on different coloured pieces of felt to be added to the stocking as decoration.

2 Cut out the stars and dots and position them on one side of the stocking. When you are happy with the positions, glue them on to the stocking and leave the glue to dry.

3 Sew the two shapes together, around the edge, to make the stocking. Fold a piece of ribbon in half to make a hanging loop and sew it into the side of the stocking.

4 Sew the bell on to the toe of the stocking. Gently shake the stocking to hear the bell make a jingling sound.

Snowstorm Shaker

Carefully shake the jam jar and watch the glitter snow twinkle! If you enjoy making this project you could make other snow jars, such as a Father Christmas or a Christmas tree.

YOU WILL NEED
modelling clay in various colours, including white
jam jar with a tight-fitting lid
cold water
silver glitter

jam jar

silver glitter

modelling clay

1 To make the snowman's head and body, roll two balls of white modelling clay in your hands. Make the ball for the snowman's body slightly bigger than the one for his head. Stick the smaller ball on top of the larger ball.

2 Make the snowman a hat and a scarf out of small pieces of different coloured modelling clay. Make him a carrot nose and a happy face.

3 Make sure your jam jar is clean, with no greasy fingerprints on it! Fill the inside of the lid with another piece of white modelling clay.

4 Use your fingers to make a shallow hole in the modelling clay on the lid. Firmly position the snowman into the hole, making sure he feels secure.

5 Pour cold water into the jam jar so that it is three-quarters full. Sprinkle in at least one tablespoon of the glitter.

6 Carefully screw on the lid and slowly turn the jar upside down, so that your snowman is the right way up. Add a little more water if needed.

Christmas Crackers

Fill these fun crackers with a small gift. Write your own jokes on small pieces of paper and tuck them inside, too.

YOU WILL NEED
small gift and joke
tissue paper in various colours
cardboard toilet paper tube
PVA (white) glue
pinking shears
paper gift ribbon
pencil
scissors
coloured paper

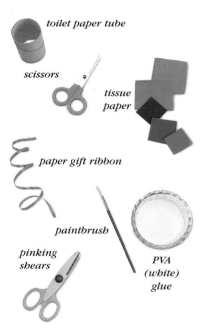

toilet paper tube

scissors

tissue paper

paper gift ribbon

paintbrush

pinking shears

PVA (white) glue

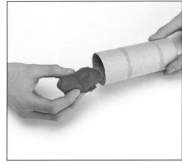

1 Neatly wrap the small gift in a piece of tissue paper and place it with your joke inside the toilet paper tube.

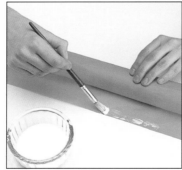

2 Cover the toilet paper tube with a large piece of tissue paper and glue the edges of the paper to hold it in place. Trim the ends with a pair of pinking shears for a decorative effect.

3 Glue a contrasting colour of tissue paper around the toilet paper tube. Tie a piece of ribbon around each end of the cracker. Pull along the length of the ribbon with a pencil to make it curl.

4 Using scissors or pinking shears, cut out a piece of paper in a fun shape. If you like, you can write the name of the person who will get the cracker on the paper. Glue the paper on to the cracker.

Party Paper Chains

Why not have a competition with your friends to see who can make the longest paper chain? Decorate your bedroom and use up leftover scraps of paper at the same time!

YOU WILL NEED
pencil
coloured paper
paintbrush
poster paints in various colours
glitter glue
scissors
PVA (white) glue

glitter glue

coloured paper

paintbrush

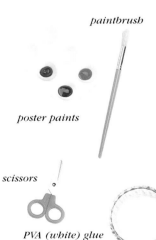

poster paints

scissors

PVA (white) glue

1 Make your own template for the paper chain, as long or as wide as you want. Draw around the template on a piece of coloured paper so that the strips are next to each other. Don't cut the strips out yet.

2 Paint your paper chain strips with lots of bright colours and fun swirls, stripes and dots. Allow the paint to dry.

3 If you like you can add a few dabs of glitter glue to the strips for extra sparkle. Allow the glitter to dry. Cut out all of the decorated strips of paper.

4 Curl the first strip of paper around so you can glue one end of the strip to the other. Hold it while the glue dries. Thread a second strip of paper through the first loop and glue the ends together. Continue until the chain is really long!

Felt Tree Calendar

This calendar is quick and easy to make and looks lovely hung on the wall. It will also make a very useful present, if you don't mind giving it away!

YOU WILL NEED
felt-tip pen
scissors
felt squares in various colours
fabric scissors
PVA (white) glue
paintbrush
mirror tile sequins
thin cardboard
mini calendar
ribbon

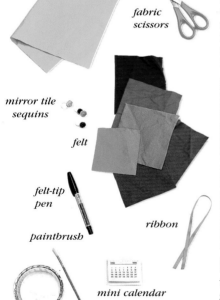

felt

fabric scissors

mirror tile sequins

felt

felt-tip pen

ribbon

paintbrush

mini calendar

PVA (white) glue

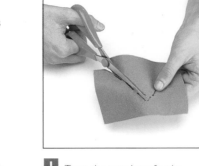

1 Trace the templates for the Christmas tree from this book and cut them out. Place the templates on the felt, draw around them and cut them out using fabric scissors. Save the leftover pieces of felt for other projects.

2 Using a pair of fabric scissors, snip a decorative fringe along the bottom edge of each section of the tree.

3 To make the background for your tree, cut out a large piece of felt. Glue on the fringed sections of felt to make the Christmas tree.

4 Glue a few mirror tile sequins on to each section of the Christmas tree to give it a bit of sparkle.

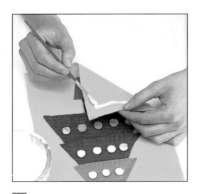

5 To make the background for your felt picture, cut out a piece of thin cardboard to the size you want. Glue the cardboard on the picture. Leave to dry.

6 Glue the calendar underneath your picture. Fold a piece of ribbon in half to make a hanging loop and stick it on to the back of the cardboard at the top. Leave the glue to dry.

Groovy Party Hats

Wearing one of these wacky hats at a Christmas party will definitely make you the envy of all of your friends.

YOU WILL NEED
pencil
scissors
coloured cardboard
paper fasteners
coloured paper
crêpe paper
ribbon
double-sided sticky tape
PVA (white) glue
paintbrush
mini pom-poms or tinsel

coloured cardboard

coloured paper

mini pom-poms

paper fasteners

PVA (white) glue and paintbrush

scissors

ribbon

crêpe paper

1 Trace the template for the party hat from this book, scale it up and cut it out. Draw around the template on a large piece of coloured cardboard. Cut out the hat shape and roll it into a cone. Hold the cone shape in place with the paper fasteners.

2 Cut out some circles from the coloured paper. You will need circles in two different sizes and a heart shape. Make other fun shapes, such as stars, if you like.

3 Starting with the large circle, place the smaller circle on top and then the heart. Pierce a paper fastener through the shapes. Make a small hole in the hat and place the paper fastener through it.

4 Open out the paper fastener so that it lies flat on the inside of the hat. Roll a piece of crêpe paper into a tight roll and place it in the top of the hat. Using a pair of scissors, snip into the top of the crêpe paper to turn it into a tassel.

5 Measure around the base of the hat and cut a length of ribbon long enough to go around it. Using a strip of double-sided sticky tape or glue, stick the ribbon around the base of the hat.

6 Glue mini pom-poms or tinsel on to the ribbon around the base of the hat. Allow the glue to dry completely before trying on your new hat.

Glittery Gift Boxes

These spectacular little gift boxes look very impressive, but are very simple to make.

YOU WILL NEED
pencil
small paper bauble (styrofoam ball)
paintbrush
poster paints in various colours
fabric scissors
squares of felt in red and green
PVA (white) glue
small cardboard boxes
glitter in various colours
mini pom-poms
small glass beads in various colours

cardboard box

paper bauble (styrofoam ball)

glitter

PVA (white) glue

glass beads

pencil

paintbrush

poster paints

1 Using a pencil, lightly draw the outline of whipped cream on a Christmas pudding (cake) on to the paper bauble (styrofoam ball).

2 Paint the base of the pudding brown and allow the paint to dry. Paint small black raisins on the brown paint to make your pudding look tasty! Leave the paint to dry.

3 Use fabric scissors to cut out two mini holly leaves from a piece of green felt, then cut two small circles of red felt for the berries. Using just a tiny dot of glue, glue the holly leaves and berries on to the top of the painted pudding.

4 Glue the Christmas pudding on to the lid of the gift box. Allow the glue to dry completely.

5 Using a glue brush, paint glue all around the pudding and sprinkle on the glitter. Lightly tap the lid on a work surface to remove any excess glitter.

6 Another fun way to decorate a gift box is to glue a mini pom-pom on to the lid, then paint on glue around the pom-pom and sprinkle small glass beads all over it for a sparkly effect.

Winter Wonderland

This little tree scene is really magical and makes a beautiful table decoration. You can enjoy watching the trees twinkle in the light.

YOU WILL NEED
pine cone
cork
strong glue
acrylic paint in various colours
paintbrush
PVA (white) glue
glitter in various colours
coloured cardboard
scissors
small cardboard box

box

cork

pine cone

strong glue

glitter

acrylic paint

paintbrush

1 Make sure your pine cone is clean and dry. Glue the base of the pine cone on to the top of a cork using strong glue. Firmly hold the cone and the cork together for a few minutes until the glue has dried completely.

2 When the glue is dry, hold the cork in your hand and gently paint the pine cone. Stand the cork upright to allow the paint on the cone to dry.

3 Paint the cork in a different colour, holding the pine cone. Allow the paint to dry.

4 Using a glue brush, paint PVA (white) glue all over the pine cone.

5 Sprinkle glitter over the cone and then tap the cork to remove the excess glitter. Cut a small star out of cardboard and glue it to the top of the cone.

6 Decorate a small gift box by gluing the glittery pine cone tree on to the lid.

PRESENTS

Wintry Scarf and Gloves

This designer set of accessories is sure to keep chilly winds at bay, and you can be sure that no-one else will own such an eye-catching set.

YOU WILL NEED
felt-tip pen
scissors
felt squares in various colours
fabric scissors
scarf
pins
needle
embroidery thread (floss) in
   various colours
small glass beads
mini pom-poms
gloves
pinking shears

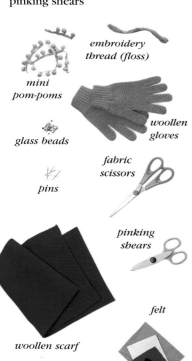

embroidery thread (floss)

mini pom-poms

glass beads

woollen gloves

pins

fabric scissors

pinking shears

felt

woollen scarf

1 Trace the templates from this book and cut them out. Draw around the snowman's head and body on a piece of white felt and cut them out. Pin the snowman to one of the ends of the scarf and sew him on.

2 Using the templates, cut the snowman's carrot nose, hat, scarf and arms out of different coloured pieces of felt.

3 Position the shapes on the snowman. When you are happy with the shapes, pin them down and sew them in place.

4 Sew a few beads down the front of the snowman's body for buttons and two on the face for eyes.

5 Position a mini pom-pom on the tip of the snowman's hat and sew it in place. Sew more pom-poms around the snowman and over the scarf to look like little snowballs.

6 For the gloves, cut two large and two small stars out of felt, using pinking shears if you like. Sew one large star onto each glove. Sew the small star on to the large star. Sew on a few beads and add a pom-pom.

Christmas Message Board

This is the perfect present to give to a grown-up, especially if they are the type of person who is always losing important pieces of paper! You might find it useful to have an extra pair of hands to help you fix the ribbons in place.

YOU WILL NEED
fabric scissors
large piece of green felt
ruler
cork message board
PVA (white) glue
paintbrush
ribbons
coloured drawing pins
felt-tip pen
dark green felt

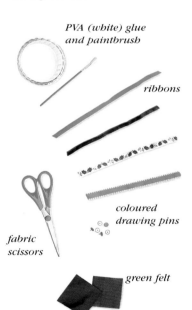

PVA (white) glue and paintbrush

ribbons

coloured drawing pins

fabric scissors

green felt

1 Cut a piece of green felt to be 5 cm (2 in) larger around each edge than the cork message board. Lay the board on top of the felt, fold the felt over the back of the board and then glue the felt firmly in place.

2 Cut lengths of ribbon and lay them diagonally across the board, spacing them at even intervals. Pin the ribbons on to the back of the message board.

3 Trace the holly leaf template from this book and cut it out. Draw around the template on a piece of dark green felt and cut out the shape. Repeat so that you have about sixteen holly leaves.

4 Using red drawing pins, pin the ends of the holly leaves to the board where the ribbons cross over, so that they look like holly berries.

Christmas Hair Slides

These make brilliant presents for anyone with long hair. They are made using neoprene which is a very light, foam-like fabric that is easy to cut. It can be bought from most specialist craft shops.

YOU WILL NEED
pencil
scrap paper
neoprene sheets in various
   colours
scissors
hair slide (barrette)
strong glue
artificial gemstones

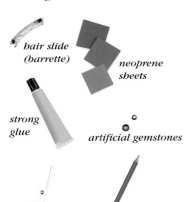

*hair slide
(barrette)*

*neoprene
sheets*

*strong
glue*

artificial gemstones

scissors

pencil

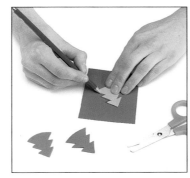

1 Draw a simple Christmas tree shape on a piece of scrap paper and cut it out to make a template. Draw around the template on the neoprene and cut out. Repeat to make six tree shapes.

2 Cut out a strip of neoprene to fit over the hair slide (barrette) and fix it in place with strong glue. You might need to hold the neoprene in place with your hands while the glue dries.

3 Glue the shapes on the hair slide with strong glue. Allow the glue to dry before trying on the hair slide.

4 You can also jazz up a plain headband with cut-out neoprene shapes such as stars. Pile on the glamour by gluing an artificial gemstone on to the centre of each star.

Father Christmas Puppet

Put on your own Christmas puppet show by making your own puppets. This project shows you how to make a Father Christmas, but why not try making a snowman or a fairy puppet, too?

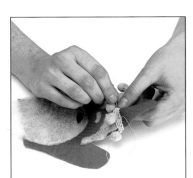

YOU WILL NEED
pencil
scrap paper
felt squares in red, pink
 and pale pink
fabric scissors
wadding (batting) fabric
pins
needle
sewing thread
small glass beads
pom-pom trim
small bell

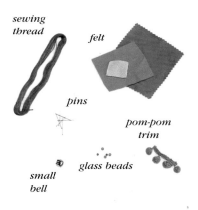

sewing thread
felt
pins
pom-pom trim
glass beads
small bell

1 Draw a glove puppet shape on scrap paper and cut it out to make a template. Position the template on red felt and cut out two puppet shapes. Cut a beard, moustache and eyebrows from the wadding (batting) fabric and pin them on to one of the puppet shapes.

2 Thread the needle with sewing thread and start to sew the wadding in place on the puppet. Remove the pins when you have finished sewing.

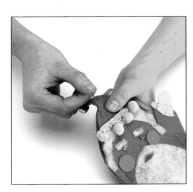

3 Sew a length of pom-pom trim just above the eyebrows.

4 Sew a blue bead under each eyebrow. Draw a hand shape on pale pink felt and cut it out. Draw two small circles for the cheeks on pink felt and cut them out.

5 Sew the hand in place on the thumb of the glove and sew the cheeks on either side of the face. Place the two puppet shapes together and pin in place.

6 Sew the bell on to the top of the puppet. Sew around the edge of the glove, leaving the bottom edge open to fit your hand in. Try on the glove and hear the bell jingle as Santa moves about!

Decoupage Santa Tray

Have some fun designing your own breakfast tray: it makes a great present and you could design it to suit whoever you are giving it to. The tray here would be great for a brother or sister.

YOU WILL NEED
fine sandpaper
small wooden tray
damp cloth
acrylic paint in various colours
paintbrushes
scissors
wrapping paper
PVA (white) glue
glitter glue
sequins
water-based clear varnish

sequins

scissors

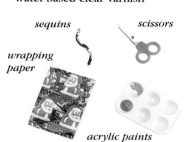

wrapping paper

acrylic paints

sandpaper

paintbrushes

wooden tray

PVA (white) glue

1 To prepare the tray for painting, rub it all over with fine sandpaper to make sure the surface is completely smooth and there are no rough areas. Wipe away any dust with a damp cloth. Leave the tray to dry.

2 On a well-covered surface, paint the tray all over. Allow the paint to dry. For best results you may need to cover the tray with two coats of paint.

3 Cut out your favourite pictures from the wrapping paper and position the pictures on the tray. When you are happy with them, stick them on with glue. Allow the glue to dry completely.

4 Add a few dabs of paint or glitter glue around the pictures to give the tray an extra sparkle. Leave to dry.

5 Using a fine paintbrush, and a contrasting colour of paint, paint the edge of the tray with narrow stripes. Leave the paint to dry.

6 Glue some sequins on the tray and leave for several minutes to allow the glue to dry. Using a varnishing brush, paint on a few coats of clear varnish. Allow the varnish to dry.

Mini Gift Bags

These little bags are ideal for putting a small gift inside. You could also hang them up on the Christmas tree, filled with tempting chocolates.

YOU WILL NEED
ruler
fabric
fabric scissors
felt square
ribbon
needle
sewing thread
embroidery thread (floss)
braid
cord
safety pin

sewing thread
cord
ribbon
felt
braid
fabric
embroidery thread (floss)
fabric scissors

1 Cut a piece of fabric measuring 20 cm (8 in) × 15 cm (6 in) and a length of ribbon 18 cm (7 in). Trace the template from this book and cut it out. Cut around the template with fabric scissors, to make a star from the felt.

2 Sew the ribbon along one edge of the fabric 1 cm (½ in) from the top. Sew along each side of the ribbon but leave the ends open.

3 Sew the felt star on to one side of the fabric. If you don't want to do too much sewing, you could glue the star on with a small dab of glue.

4 Fold the fabric in half with the right sides facing, making sure that all four corners meet. Carefully sew a running stitch along the bottom and side of the bag, using embroidery thread (floss). When you have finished sewing the bag, turn it the right way out.

5 Cut a piece of braid to go around the top of the bag and sew it in place with a running stitch.

6 Cut a length of cord and secure a safety pin through one end. Thread the cord through the ribbon at the top of the bag, until it comes out at the other end. Tie the two ends in a knot. Pull the cord tight to close the bag.

Funky Egg Cups

These jazzy egg cups will add lots of fun and colour to the breakfast table all year round. Make a special friend their own, personalized egg cup by painting on their name.

YOU WILL NEED
enamel paints in various colours
paintbrushes
china egg cups
coloured paper or
    wrapping paper
scissors
PVA (white) glue

china egg cup

PVA (white) glue

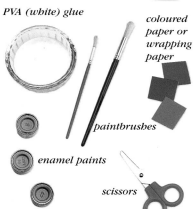

coloured paper or wrapping paper

paintbrushes

enamel paints

scissors

1 If you have more than one egg cup, you can give each one a different design. Paint stripes on one egg cup in a single colour. Paint slowly and carefully, and try to leave even spaces between the stripes. Allow the paint to dry.

2 Paint on some more stripes in different colours. Allow the paint to dry completely, then paint the inside of the egg cup in a single colour. Leave to dry.

3 For the tartan (plaid) egg cup, paint stripes in one colour and allow the paint to dry. In another colour, paint more stripes in the other direction and leave to dry. Paint the inside of the egg cup.

4 For the third egg cup, paint the inside and outside in contrasting colours. Let dry. Cut small squares from coloured paper or wrapping paper and glue them on. To finish, dab white paint over the egg cup to look like snow. Leave to dry.

Traditional Pomander

This is a beautiful Christmas decoration that has a subtle, spicy perfume. It would make an ideal gift for a grown-up.

YOU WILL NEED
ribbon
orange
scissors
cloves
PVA (white) glue
paintbrush
gold glitter

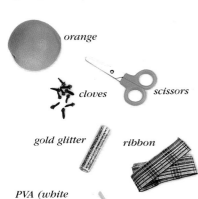

orange

cloves   *scissors*

gold glitter   *ribbon*

PVA (white glue)   *paintbrush*

1 Holding the orange in your fingers, wrap the length of ribbon tightly around the orange. Keep hold of the ribbon.

2 Without letting go of the ribbon, twist it and wrap it around the orange in the other direction. Tie the ribbon in a large bow at the top and trim the ends.

3 Cover the whole orange with cloves by carefully piercing the pointed ends of the cloves into the orange.

4 Brush a thin layer of glue over the cloves and sprinkle glitter over the orange, shaking off any of the excess. Let the glue dry.

Christmas Pudding Apron

This apron looks delicious! As well as painting Christmas puddings, you could paint your favourite Christmas foods.

YOU WILL NEED
cardboard
scourer pad (sponge)
felt-tip pen
scissors
fabric paint in assorted colours
cotton apron
paintbrush

cardboard

fabric paint

scissors

felt-tip pen

cotton apron

scourer pad (sponge)

paintbrush

1 Trace the Christmas pudding (cake) template from this book, cut it out and draw around it on to cardboard. Cut out the pudding shape and draw around it on a scourer pad (sponge), using a felt-tip pen. With the help of an adult, cut the pudding out of the scourer pad.

2 Dab the sponge side of the scourer pad with purple fabric paint and make a practice stamp on a scrap of fabric. Then dab the sponge in the paint and stamp puddings all over the apron, dabbing the sponge in the paint after each print.

3 Trace the holly leaf template from this book, cut it out and draw around it on to cardboard. Carefully cut out the cardboard inside the leaf to make a stencil. Position the stencil on the top of each pudding and dab the sponge, dipped in green paint, through it. Let dry.

4 Paint some white paint on to the top of the puddings to look like whipped cream. Allow to dry.

5 Using red paint, paint some red dots on to each pudding to look like glacé (candied) cherries. Allow to dry.

6 Finish the puddings by painting two red dots next to the holly leaves to look like festive berries.

Christmas Pudding Teapot

An ordinary cup of tea will never be the same again when served from this quirky teapot! You might need to paint on two coats of white paint, but remember to allow the first coat to dry before painting on the second layer.

YOU WILL NEED
small brown teapot
tissues
paintbrushes
ceramic paints in various colours

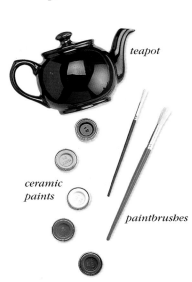

teapot

ceramic paints

paintbrushes

1 Before you start painting, wipe the teapot with tissues to remove all traces of grease and dirt. Leave the teapot to dry before you start to paint.

2 Remove the lid from the teapot. Paint the white "cream" on the teapot lid and around the top of the pot. Allow the paint to dry.

3 Paint black and brown dots on the unpainted area of the teapot to look like currants and raisins.

4 Paint the knob on the teapot lid red to look like a glacé (candied) cherry. Allow the paint to dry.

Snowman Mug

Warm up this chilly snowman with a nice cup of piping hot chocolate or tea!

YOU WILL NEED
mug
tissues
paintbrushes
ceramic paints in assorted
   colours

mug

paintbrushes

ceramic paints

1   Before you start painting, wipe the mug with tissues to remove all traces of grease and dirt. Leave the mug to dry before you start to paint.

2   Using white paint, paint the snowman's head and body on the mug. Add white dots all around the snowman, to look like falling flakes of snow. Allow the paint to dry.

3   Using orange and blue paints, paint a carrot for the snowman's nose and give him a thick woolly scarf. Allow the paint to dry.

4   Using black paint, paint on the snowman's hat, his arms and charcoal eyes. Allow the paint to dry.

Jazzy Jewel Cookie Jar

This is a great idea for making an ordinary glass container look really special. All you need are some glass paints and a handful of artificial gemstones.

YOU WILL NEED

pencil
scrap paper or cardboard
scissors
sticky-backed plastic (contact paper)
glass container with a lid
paintbrush
glass paints in various colours
strong glue
artificial gemstones in various colours
gold outline paint

gold outline paint

strong glue

glass container

artificial gemstones

paintbrush

sticky-backed plastic (contact paper)

glass paints

1 Draw a star shape on a piece of scrap paper or cardboard and cut it out to make a template. Draw around the template on the sticky-backed plastic (contact paper) and cut it out. Repeat so that you have about eight stars.

2 Decide where you want to position the stars on the glass container. When you are happy with them, peel off the backing and stick them in place.

3 Paint the jar and its lid all over with glass paint. It doesn't matter if you paint over the stars, too. Allow the paint to dry completely.

4 When you are sure the paint has dried, peel the stars off the jar to reveal the unpainted stars underneath.

5 Using strong glue, stick an artificial gemstone in the centre of each star. Hold it in position for a few minutes until the glue dries.

6 Using the gold outline paint, decorate the edge of each star. The paint comes in a tube, so it is easy to control. Allow the paint to dry.

Appliquéd Photo Album

As well as decorating an album, you could also decorate the cover of a diary or an address book in a matching design.

YOU WILL NEED
pencil
scissors
felt squares in lilac and red
pinking shears
pins
needle
sewing thread
rick-rack braid
gold gauzy fabric
red velvet
poster paints in various colours
paintbrushes
yellow embroidery thread (floss)
tinsel ribbon
gold braid
star sequins
PVA (white) glue
fabric-covered album

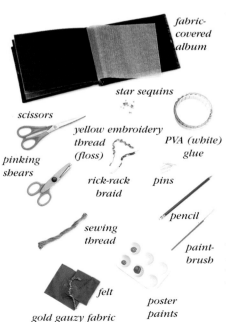

fabric-covered album

star sequins

scissors

yellow embroidery thread (floss)

PVA (white) glue

pinking shears

rick-rack braid

pins

sewing thread

pencil

paint-brush

felt

gold gauzy fabric

poster paints

1 Trace the templates and cut them out. Draw around the background template on lilac felt and cut it out. Using pinking shears, cut out a larger square from the red felt. Sew the lilac felt on to the red felt. Pin rick-rack braid all around the edge of the lilac felt.

2 Using a small, neat running stitch, sew the rick-rack braid in place around the edge of the lilac felt.

3 Using the wing template, cut out two pieces of gold fabric. Cut a piece of red velvet to the size of the dress template. Arrange the wings behind the dress shape on the lilac felt. Sew all around the edge of the wings.

4 Cut a small circle using the template for the face and paint on the eyes, rosy cheeks and a mouth. When the paint is dry, arrange the face at the top of the triangle and sew it in place.

5 For the angel's hair, sew strands of embroidery thread (floss) to the top of her head. Sew a piece of tinsel ribbon on to her hair to look like a halo. Sew a piece of gold braid along the bottom of her dress. Sew star sequins over her dress and circular sequins on her wings. Using a small amount of glue, secure the appliqué on to the front of the album. Allow the glue to dry.

Sparkly Pen Pot

These glitzy containers are great for storing pens and pencils. Remember to ask your friends and family to keep all their foil sweet (candy) wrappers, so that you can make a whole range of containers.

YOU WILL NEED
plastic bottle
felt-tip pen
scissors
ruler
cardboard
foil sweet (candy) wrappers
PVA (white) glue
paintbrush
double-sided sticky tape
mini pom-poms

PVA (white) glue

paintbrush

mini pom-poms

scissors

ruler

cardboard

foil sweet (candy) wrappers

plastic bottle

double-sided sticky tape

1 Decide on the height you want your container to be and draw a line around the bottle with a felt-tip pen to mark this. Ask an adult to help you cut the top off the bottle.

2 Measure the height of the bottle with a ruler. Allowing for a 2 cm (¾ in) overlap, cut out a piece of cardboard to fit around it.

3 Select a colourful assortment of foil sweet (candy) wrappers and smooth them out with your fingers until they are flat. Prepare enough wrappers to cover your container.

4 Glue the foil sweet wrappers on to one side of the cardboard until you have completely covered the surface. For the best pattern effect, let the wrappers overlap each other. Allow the glue to dry.

5 Stick strips of double-sided sticky tape on to the reverse side of the cardboard. Peel off the backing tape and fix the cardboard around the bottle.

6 For the finishing touch, decorate the top of the container by gluing on a selection of mini pom-poms.

Holly Leaf Picture Frame

Jazz up an old picture frame with this simple technique, using tiling grout. Put a photograph of your favourite friend in the frame, then display it, so that everyone can appreciate your handiwork.

YOU WILL NEED
fine sandpaper
wooden picture frame
damp cloth
ruler
white pencil
paintbrush
acrylic paints in various colours
pencil
cardboard
scissors
tiling grout
old spoon

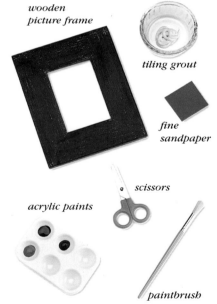

wooden picture frame

tiling grout

fine sandpaper

acrylic paints

scissors

paintbrush

1 Using the sandpaper, lightly rub down the picture frame to remove any old paint or varnish, and to smooth the surface. Using a damp cloth, wipe over the frame to remove any dirt or dust.

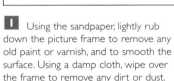

2 Using a ruler and a white pencil, divide the picture frame into squares.

3 Paint on the squares as neatly as possible. Allow the paint to dry. You may find it easier to paint one colour and allow it to dry before painting on a new colour.

4 Trace the holly leaf template from this book and cut it out. Draw around the template on a piece of cardboard. With the help of an adult, cut out the inside leaf to make a stencil.

5 Squeeze a small amount of grout into an old container and add a small amount of paint. Using an old spoon, mix the paint into the grout until the colour is evenly mixed.

6 When the paint is dry, position the stencil on a painted square and thickly dab the coloured grout through it: it will give a lovely ridged effect to the frame. Remove the stencil and repeat on the other squares. Allow the grout to dry

Snowflake Candlestick

Decide on who you want to give this candlestick to and then you can paint it in their favourite colours. If you like, you could also give them a Christmas candle to go with it.

YOU WILL NEED
fine sandpaper
plain ceramic candlestick
scissors
sticky-backed plastic
   (contact paper)
enamel paints in various colours
paintbrush
gold ceramic paint

enamel paint

gold ceramic paint

fine sandpaper

scissors

ceramic candlestick

sticky-backed plastic (contact paper)

paintbrush

1 Using fine sandpaper, lightly rub down the candlestick to remove the glaze. This will make it easier to paint on to the candlestick.

2 Cut out small circles and strips from the sticky-backed plastic (contact paper). Stick the strips across the upper part of the candlestick and the circles around the base of the candlestick.

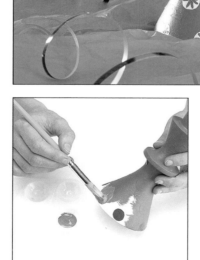

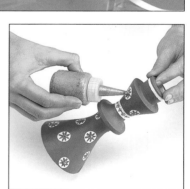

3 Paint the candlestick. Allow the paint to dry completely, then remove the sticky-backed plastic shapes.

4 Paint a snowflake inside each circle and allow to dry. Then, using the gold paint, dot the centre of each snowflake to make your candlestick twinkle.

Hair Scrunchies

This is the perfect present for someone who likes to wear their hair tied back. Use fabrics that you know will match their hair colour. You could also make two smaller scrunchies for someone who likes to wear their hair in pigtails.

YOU WILL NEED
fabric 65 cm (26 in) x 14 cm (5½ in)
ruler
fabric scissors
pins
needle
sewing thread
thin elastic
safety pin

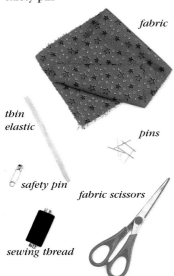

fabric

thin elastic

pins

safety pin

fabric scissors

sewing thread

1 Fold the fabric in half lengthways, making sure that the right sides of the fabric are facing. Carefully pin the two edges together, then sew a neat running stitch along the long edge.

2 Turn the fabric tube right side out. Cut a piece of thin elastic 18 cm (7 in) long. Secure a safety pin through one end of the elastic. Using the safety pin to help, thread the elastic all the way through the fabric tube.

3 When the elastic comes out of the other end of the tube, remove the safety pin and pin the two ends of elastic together. Sew the ends together.

4 Turn under the raw edges of one end of the tube and pin over the other end. Sew the two together, taking care not to sew right through the scrunchie.

Friendship Bracelets

Give one of your friends or someone in your family one of these special bracelets, to show them just how much you care about them.

YOU WILL NEED
stranded cotton embroidery
  thread (floss) in various colours
ruler
scissors
strong sticky tape
beads in various colours

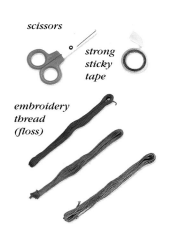

scissors

*strong
sticky
tape*

*embroidery
thread
(floss)*

1 Decide on four colours of embroidery thread (floss) and cut two strands of each colour approximately 40 cm (16 in) long. Tie all of the strands together in a knot at one of the ends.

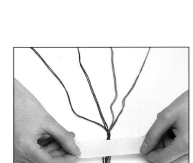

2 Using a strong piece of sticky tape, stick the strands on a flat surface just above the knot. Lay out the threads as shown.

3 Take the first pair of coloured threads on the right and knot them over the pair of threads on the left.

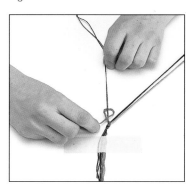

4 Tie another knot and then go on to the next pair of threads and tie two knots. Continue until you get to the end of the row.

5 Go back to the new thread on the left and continue the same technique, as in step 3. Keep knotting until the bracelet is long enough to fit around the wrist of the person it will be given to.

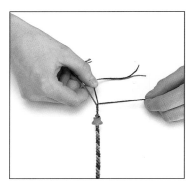

6 Divide the threads into three sections and plait (braid) them together. Thread on a bead and then tie a knot at the end, to hold the bead in place. Trim off any trailing strands.

Festive Dog Bowl

Don't forget to make your pets a present at Christmas time. If you have a cat, why not make a cat bowl instead? You'll find a fish bone template here in this book to decorate it with.

YOU WILL NEED
felt-tip pen
scissors
cardboard
masking tape
metal dog bowl
sponge
enamel paints in various colours
tissue
paintbrush
strong glue
artificial gemstones

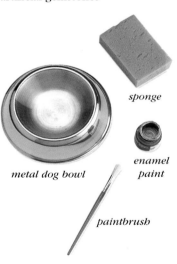

sponge

metal dog bowl

enamel paint

paintbrush

1 Trace the template for the dog bone from this book and cut it out. Draw around the template on a piece of cardboard.

2 Carefully cut out the inside of the bone shape to make a stencil. You may need the help of an adult to do this.

3 Hold the stencil firmly against the bowl or, if you find it easier, fix it to the side of the bowl with a piece of masking tape. Using a sponge, dab paint through the stencil on to the bowl. Repeat all the way around the bowl.

4 Neaten up the edges of the bones with a tissue. Leave the paint to dry.

5 Paint an outline around each bone in a contrasting colour of paint.

6 Using strong glue, stick the artificial gemstones on the bowl, between each of the bones.

Royal Party Crown

Make your parents a king and queen for the day by giving them this fabulous golden crown to wear. Make one for your Christmas parties, too.

YOU WILL NEED
pencil
scrap paper
scissors
gold cardboard
PVA (white) glue
artificial gemstones
glitter glue
paper fasteners
double-sided sticky tape
tinsel

glitter glue

paper fasteners

gold cardboard

PVA (white) glue and paintbrush

artificial gemstones

tinsel

double-sided sticky tape

1 Draw a crown shape on a piece of scrap paper and cut it out to make a template. Make sure the crown will be the right size for your head when the ends are joined together. Draw round the template on gold cardboard.

2 Using PVA (white) glue, stick the artificial gemstones on to the crown. Leave until the glue is dry.

3 Using glitter glue, carefully highlight the edge of the crown. Leave to dry.

4 Join the ends of the crown together, adjusting the size to fit your head, and secure in place with the paper fasteners.

5 Stick a strip of double-sided sticky tape around the base of the crown.

6 Peel the paper backing off the sticky tape and press on the tinsel, all the way around the crown.

Christmas Tree Earrings

These festive earrings will certainly make you stand out at a party. They clip on, so you don't even have to have pierced ears to wear them.

YOU WILL NEED
felt-tip pen
scissors
cardboard
gummed tape
paintbrush
gold paint
foil paper in various colours
PVA (white) glue
sequins
sewing thread
strong glue
clip-on earring findings

PVA (white) glue and paintbrush

foil paper

gold paint

sewing thread

cardboard

paintbrush

gummed tape

sequins

scissors

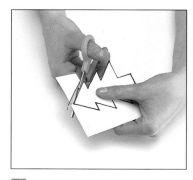

1 Trace the earring templates from this book and cut them out. Draw around the templates on a piece of cardboard. You will need to cut out two Christmas trees and two circles for each pair of earrings.

2 Tear up small pieces of gummed tape and dampen the back of them to make them sticky. Stick them on to both of the circle and Christmas tree shapes.

3 When the paper has dried, paint the shapes gold. Allow the paint to dry.

4 Cut out a tree shape slightly smaller than the cardboard tree from the coloured foil. Glue the shape on to the cardboard tree.

5 Add the decorations to the tree by gluing on a few sequins. Ask an adult to help you make a small hole at the top of the tree and at the edge of the circle, using the tip of a pair of scissors.

6 Thread a piece of thread through the hole in the circle and the hole in the tree. Tie the threads together with a small knot. Using PVA (white) glue, stick an earring finding onto the back circle part of each earring. Let the glue dry before trying on the earrings.

Party Badges

Make a party badge for your friends and family to wear on Christmas Day. Try to give each badge a different character to suit the person you are giving it to.

YOU WILL NEED
felt-tip pen
scissors
cardboard
gold paint
poster paints in various colours
paintbrush
wool (yarn)
ribbon
PVA (white) glue
mini pom-pom
star sequins
artificial gemstones
strong glue
brooch finding

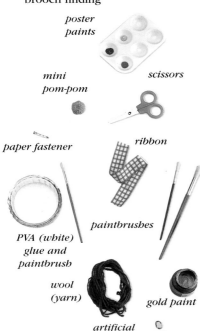

poster paints

mini pom-pom

scissors

paper fastener

ribbon

PVA (white) glue and paintbrush

paintbrushes

wool (yarn)

gold paint

artificial gemstones

1 Trace all the badge templates from this book and cut them out. Draw around the templates on a piece of cardboard and cut them out.

2 Paint the face-shaped pieces of cardboard in a flesh colour and paint the crown shape gold. Allow the paint to dry completely.

3 Using a fine paintbrush, paint the eyes, nose and mouth on the faces. Allow the paint to dry. If you find painting the details of the face too fiddly, you could use a felt-tip pen instead.

4 For the girl's hair, cut approximately nine strands of wool (yarn) to the same length. Tie them in a knot at the top and then plait (braid) them. Tie a ribbon at the end to secure the plait. You will need two plaits.

5 Glue the end of each plait to the back of the crown on either side. Allow the glue to dry. Meanwhile, paint big stripes on the boy's hat and dots on his bow tie. When the paint is dry, glue a mini pom-pom to the tip of his hat.

6 Glue the crown on to the top of the girl's head. Glue sparkly star sequins on to the crown and add artificial gemstones as a necklace. Allow the glue to dry. Using strong glue, stick a brooch finding on to the back of each badge. Leave the glue to dry.

INDEX